TEST YOUR CHIL

Spelling Practice

Frank Spooncer

About this book

The aim of this book is to help your child practise his or her spelling in order to become a good speller. Spelling is a vital skill in the English National Curriculum, and is important in all other Curriculum areas.

Although this book has the word 'test' in its title, it does not contain endless spelling lists for weary parents to read out to worried children. Tucked away at the end of the book there are three fairly formal tests which will give some idea of your child's general spelling ability. The remainder of the book, however, provides what might be called 'spelling situations', in which spelling is used as part of general English activities, rather than as a skill on its own. After all, adults do not spend time spelling isolated words: they use spelling as just one of the processes involved in putting thoughts and ideas on to paper.

The book is intended to be a family one. Although it is aimed mainly at the 7–11 age range, it should also provide activities for slightly older children, and you yourself may scratch your head over one or two items. In general, the activities become harder as the book progresses.

A book of this length cannot be comprehensive in its treatment of spelling. It does, however, provide a good sample of spelling situations to practise, which should give a guide to the spelling strengths already developed and those that have yet to be achieved. At the end of the book, there is a chart which both you and your child can use to keep a record of the progress made.

British Library Cataloguing in Publication data

Spooncer, Frank
   Spelling practice. – (Test your child)
   I. Title II. Series
   428.1

   ISBN 0-340-57045-8

This Headway edition first published 1992

© 1992 Frank Spooncer

All rights reserved. No part of this publication may be reproduced or transmitted in any form or by any means, electronic or mechanical, including photocopy, recording, or any information storage and retrieval system, without permission in writing from the publisher or under licence from the Copyright Licensing Agency Limited. Further details of such licences (for reprographic reproduction) may be obtained from the Copyright Licensing Agency Limited, of 90 Tottenham Court Road, London W1P 9HE.

Typeset by Rowland Phototypesetting Ltd, Bury St Edmunds, Suffolk

Printed in Great Britain for the educational publishing division of Hodder & Stoughton Ltd, Mill Road, Dunton Green, Sevenoaks, Kent, by C W Print Group, Loughton, Essex

Contents

1. **tch** or **ch**? **dge** or **ge**? — 4
2. **ew** or **ue**? **aw** or **au**? — 5
3. **ow** or **ou**? **ow** or **oa**? — 6
4. The wheel of fortune 1: spelling game — 7
5. Useful groups: shapes — 8
6. Fillemups 1 — 9
7. **le**, **el** or **al**? — 10
8. **ie** or **ei**? **or** or **er**? — 11
9. One and many: singulars and plurals — 12
10. Doubles and singles: words with doubled letters — 13
11. Sounds like 1 — 14
12. Endings — 15
13. Changems: spelling game — 16
14. **ti**, **ci** or **si**? — 17
15. Useful groups: animals, numbers, family words — 18
16. Fillemups 2 — 19
17. Proof reading: correcting a story — 20
18. Useful groups: days, months, seasons, time — 21
19. The wheel of fortune 2 — 22
20. Sounds like 2 — 23
21. Beginnings — 24
22. Some harder groups: zoo, hospital, food, music — 25
23. Fill it up – and put it right — 26
24. So you want some harder ones? — 27
    Spelling banks — 28
    Short test and dictation sentences — 29
    Scoring for short test and dictation sentences — 30
    Notes for parents and teachers — 31
    Progress chart — 32

1 tch or ch?

The answers to the clues given below all contain **tch** or **ch**. The first letter is given to help you each time.

Lots of money	r ...*ich*...	Rides a broomstick	w ...*itch*...
A man from Holland is	D	Boy's name	R...*obert*...
A fruit	p...*each*...	Sells meat	b...*utcher*...
Lots of fruit trees	o...*range trees*...	Food is cooked there	k...*itchen*...
A small lamp	t...*orch*...	Carries school books	s...*atchel*...
A note in music	c	'£100? Far too...'	m ....

If you fill in the answers to the clues below correctly, a **tch** word will appear, reading downwards. All the answers contain either **tch** or **ch**.

'I've never heard .... nonsense.' (s) → s u c h
Kind of long seat: used in gym (b) → b e n c h
The fielder made a great .... (c) → c a t c h
It turns lights on and off (s) → s w i t c h
Tame rabbits live in it (h) → h u t c h
More money than someone else (r) → r i c h e r

dge or ge?

Fill in the staircase using the clues given. This time, all the answers contain either **dge** or **ge**.

A diamond is one (g) → g e m
A DANGER sign was put by the cliff .... (e)
A sort of swelling (b) → b r u i s e
He was a good friend to Mole (B)
A school for older pupils (c) → c l e a n e a r
Bad cuts may need these (b) → b a n d a g e s

When you have finished the staircase, try these:

Add one letter to the answer on the first stair, to make a tiny thing that can make you ill. *germ*
Add two letters to the answer on the second stair to make something you slide on in the snow. *sledge*

2 ew or ue?

Fill the gaps in the words with either **ew** or **ue** to make sensible sentences. Simple, isn't it?

The plane fl ew in the bl ue sky.

The wind bl _ _ so the cr _ _ set the sails.

John mended the toy with gl ee and it was as good as n ew

The answers to the following clues all contain either **ew** or **ue**. The first letter and the number of letters are given.

A stone figure of someone   s tatue

Early morning water on the grass   d ue

'Sorry, but your TV payment is   d ue.'

A kind of street   a venue

You can do it to a toffee   c _ _ _

aw or au?

Now the answers must contain either **aw** or **au**.

Not cooked   r aw   Dogs have them   p aws

A short rest   p ause   To pull something   h _ _ _

Goes under a cup   s _ _ _ _ _   A month in summer   A ugust

Harvest time   A _ _ _ _ _   New boats have to be   la be ld ed

This staircase has words with **ew, ue, au** and **aw** in them.

It's used in snooker (c) → c u e
You can make this with meat and vegetables (s) → s t e w
The old book was of great .... (v) → v a l ue
You might put your socks away into this (d) → d r a w e r
He came last in the race .... he was unfit (b) →
'Look, Mum. Baby is .... on hands and knees.' (c) → c r a w l i n g

3 ow or ou?

Fill the gaps in the words with either **ow** or **ou**.

The ow̲l flew dow̲n over the tow̲er.

The clou̲d floated rou̲nd the top of the mou̲ntain.

Ou̲r new hou̲se has a sh.......er dow̲nstairs, and a big garden ou̲tside.

The lost crow̲n was worth a thou̲sand pou̲nds.

When she is cross, Jane shou̲ts, p.......ts, frow̲ns and how̲ls.

Answer the clues below with words which contain **ow** or **ou**.

Opposite of North   south
Used in the kitchen   f _ _ _ _
A loud cry   shout
We live in these   houses
Sixty minutes   hour
Shoots water in the air   f _ _ _ _ _ _ _

Grows in the garden   flower
A ball does this   bounce
Very strong   p _ _ _ _ _ _ _
One hundred new pence   pound

Here's a poem for you to complete with **ow** and **ou** words.

In the circus tent a clown...
Dressed in yellow and in brown......
Was clapped l...ou...dly by the crowd.....
'I'm so pr..oud......,' he said, al oud.......

ow or oa?

The answers to these clues all contain either **ow** or **oa**.

We wash with it   soap
A young horse   foal
Opposite of 'sink'   f _ _ _ _
It's below your chin   th _ _ _ _
Beef is often   roast

A colour   yellow
A cry when hurt   groan
Part of your arm   elbow
Another 'hurt' sound   moan
Opposite of 'wide'   narrow

4 The wheel of fortune 1

You have to make up words using one of the wheels below. The letters in the middle **must** be used each time, but you can use as many or as few of the outside letters as you like. So, in the first one, you can make **tea**, adding just one letter; or you can make **browner** from the second, using numbers 12, 4 and 3. Have a try yourself.

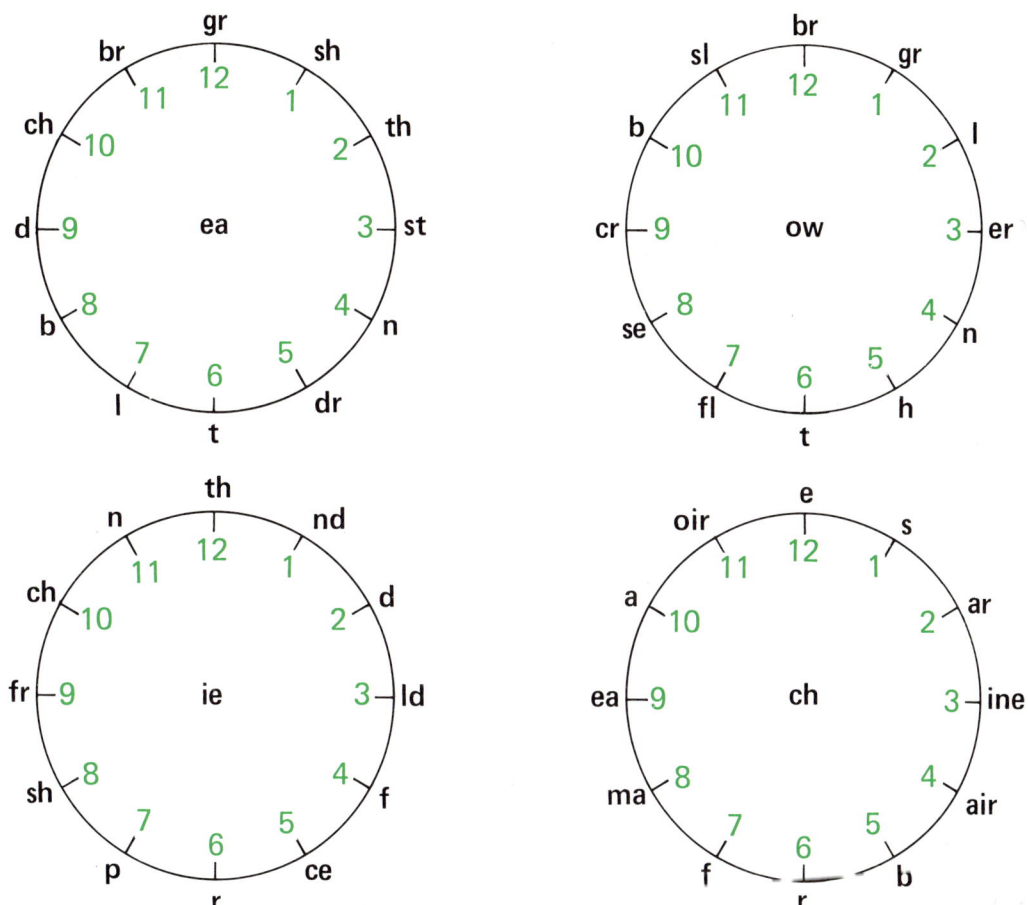

There are several different ways of playing this game. You can have a time limit, to see who can make most from one wheel; you can make the winner the one with the longest word. You can take off points for 'impossible' words, using the dictionary to check. Or you can shout out the number that begins a word; your opponent has to give the number (or numbers) of the letters that will complete a *real* word. Of course, you must have a real word in your head, in case you are challenged.

5 Useful groups: shapes

The sides of this shape are all equal. It is called a s................. From A to B is called a d ....

This shape is called a r................. From A all round the outside and back to A again is the p ....

This 'sharp' angle is called a..................

This 'blunt' one is called o..................

This 3-sided shape is a t.........................

This 6-sided shape is a h.........................

This is not an egg: but its proper name does begin with e..................................

This triangle has two equal sides. It is called an i................................ triangle.

This triangle has all three sides equal. It is called e................................

This is a c................. From A to D is the r.................. From C to B is the d.................. All the way round the outside from C and back again is the c ....

6 Fillemups 1

Fill the gaps in the words to make a sensible story. Each dash stands for a missing letter.

A picnic in the sun

The sun was h _ _, and Ratty sat on the ba _ k of the ri _ _ r. He fe _ _ very hap _ _. Mole c _ m _ up to him and said, 'Shall we t _ _ e our b _ _ t on the river?'

Ratty op _ _ ed his eyes. 'Yes, ind _ _ d we shall. We'll take s _ _ e f _ _ d to eat. I'll p _ _ k it.'

He put in br _ _ d, c _ _ _ s, sw _ _ _ s and dr _ _ k un _ _ _ the basket was f _ _ _.

'You'll s _ _ k the boat,' said M _ _ _. They r _ _ ed a little way al _ _ g to a pr _ _ _ y spot, unpacked their lu _ _ _, and sh _ _ ed it between them. After they had e _ _ _ n, they b _ _ h had a good sl _ _ p in the sun. Ratty w _ _ e first. 'T _ _ e to go, old son,' he said. 'Time to go.' 'What a sh _ _ e,' said Mole. 'But th _ _ _ you. It's been a lo _ _ _ _ afternoon.'

Put the story right

You have to correct the spelling mistakes in the story below. The first one has been done for you.

John was trieing [trying] to wright [story] a storey, but he could not get it rite. His typewriter cept speeling words rong.

'Buther it,' siad John. 'I'll sel it.'

So he tuk the mashine to the chop, and torked to the oaner. The owner soled John a mush beter machine, and John took it home. 'Now I'll bee a propper writer,' he said 'I'll be famouse and ritch.' He tipped away, but still the words apeared wrong. He shouk his haed. and said, 'I've waisted my mony. I'm the orful speler – not the machine.'

7 le, el or al?

All the answers have **le** or **el** or **al** in them.

You eat at it   t _ _ _ _
A dog lives in it   k _ _ _ _ _
He loves nuts   squ _ _ _ _ _
Flat and even   l _ _ _ _
A small church   c _ _ _ _ _
Another church   t _ _ _ _ _
Footballers do it   dr _ _ _ _ _
Swiss sing this way   y _ _ _ _

Flowers have them   p _ _ _ _ _
Barges go on them   c _ _ _ _ _
Light summer shoe   s _ _ _ _ _
For sick people   h _ _ _ _ _ _ _
Very big church   c _ _ _ _ _ _ _ _
Very quick   n _ _ _ _ _
Opposite of 'lady'   g _ _ _ _ _ _ _ _
Helps sewing   th _ _ _ _ _

Now try these puzzles:

Find a word of 6 letters, starts with **s**, means 'easy' ....
Change one letter for a word meaning 'an example' ....
A word of 5 letters, starts with **a**, part of a triangle ....
Change 2 letters around for something with wings ....

In this 'crossword' there are (at least) eleven words that contain **le** or **el** or **al**. They all read either across or down. Try to find the words – but be careful. There are some words put in to trick you – they are not spelt properly!

T	R	O	U	B	L	E	P	M	E
E	S	S	I	M	P	A	L	U	M
S	C	C	A	N	A	L	E	D	O
G	A	R	B	L	E	D	A	D	O
E	N	I	S	S	I	N	G	L	E
N	D	B	M	I	D	D	E	L	L
T	A	B	E	L	L	E	N	E	B
E	L	L	O	M	A	N	T	L	E
L	S	E	V	E	R	A	L	E	L
E	S	C	A	R	A	M	E	L	E

....
....
....
....
....
....
....
....
....
....

Any more?

8 ie or ei?

In this first group, **ie** and **ei** stand for similar sounds. Choose the right one to form words that fit the clues.

Horses graze in it   f _ _ _ _   Lights hang from it   c _ _ _ _ _ _

A boy's name   N _ _ _   A loud shout   sh _ _ _ _

To grab hold of   s _ _ _ _   Proud and vain   con _ _ _ _ _ _

Very short   br _ _ _   A Knight carried it   sh _ _ _ _

Sorrow   gr _ _ _   Given when a bill is paid   r _ _ _ _ _ _

But sometimes, **ie** and **ei** can represent other sounds. Try these:

Santa rides one   s _ _ _ _ _   Opposite of enemy   f _ _ _ _ _

Very strange   w _ _ _ _   Lives next door   n _ _ _ _ _ _ _ _

A wicked person   f _ _ _ _   Used to steer horse   r _ _ _

A King does this   r _ _ _ _ _   Very naughty   mi _ _ _ _ _ _ _ _ _

or or er?

The letters **or** and **er** are often used at the ends of words to do with what people do, just as **collector** stands for someone who collects things. Answer these clues with **or** or **er** words.

A person who acts .... Someone who teaches ....

Someone who works .... Invents things ....

Gives lectures .... Inspects ....

To do with law (6) .... Writes books (a,6) ....

Survives .... Sells vegetables (g,11) ....

Relations, long ago (a,9) .... Betrays his country (t,7) ....

An unmarried man (b,8) .... Competes (10) ....

Gives sermons in church (p,8) ....

An unmarried woman (sp,8) ....

9 One and many

Here are some words we use when there is just one thing, like one **cat** or one **cheese**. Write down the spellings you would use if there were many. (You probably know they are called PLURALS.)

hat .... house .... prize .... tray ....
sea .... rag .... model .... gift ....
coach .... match .... pass .... wash ....
bus .... boss .... tomato .... domino ....
elf .... wolf .... half .... chief ....
wife .... roof .... thief .... shelf ....
baby .... lady .... valley .... fly ....
supply .... sheep .... berry .... woman ....
tooth .... child .... holiday ....
chimney ....

This time, you have to write down the spelling you would use if there was only one thing: the SINGULAR.

mazes .... foxes .... waves .... gloves ....
hooves .... calves .... potatoes .... peaches ....
heroes .... replies .... scarves .... lives ....
lambs .... crashes .... gypsies .... lilies ....
churches .... penalties ....
balloons .... countries ....

Walk down these stairs (or you can climb them if you like). All the answers are plurals.

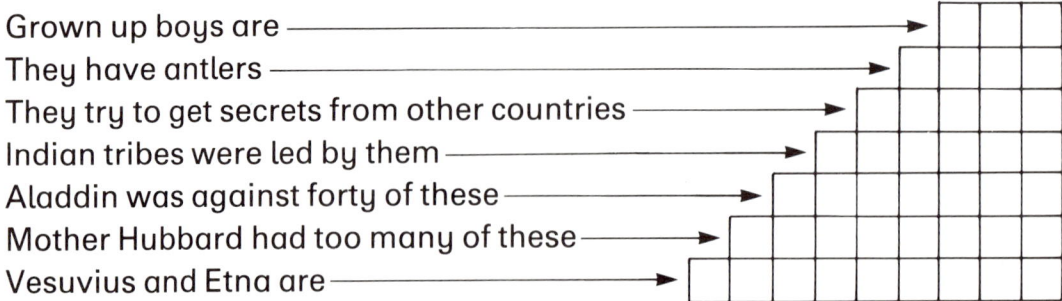

Grown up boys are
They have antlers
They try to get secrets from other countries
Indian tribes were led by them
Aladdin was against forty of these
Mother Hubbard had too many of these
Vesuvius and Etna are

10 Doubles and singles

Many words have a doubled letter in them, as in pu**dd**ing. The clues below are for words which have at least one doubled letter in them – but which one is it? To help you, the first letter, and the number of letters, are given.

To knock nails in (h,6) .... Larger (b,6) ....

Hot drink (c,6) .... Makes canoes move (p,6) ....

Reddish vegetable (c,6) .... Green vegetable (c,7) ....

An argument (q,7) .... To argue (sq,8) ....

On an envelope (a,7) .... Made of wool (w,7) ....

Not the same (d,9) .... Vanish (d,9) ....

A mistake (e,5) .... Not guilty (i,8) ....

Another word for 'burglar' (r,6) ....

Yellow flower in Spring (d,8) ....

The start of something (b,9) ....

An Army major is one (o,7) ....

To give in (e.g. in war) (s,9) ....

Very, very good (e,9) ....

You might find this one easier. Put a **single** or a **double** letter in each box to make sensible sentences.

'Begi☐ at the begi☐ing,' said the Mad Ha☐er.
Ha☐y was ho☐ing Ma☐y would stop ho☐ing
'You are a☐ways we☐come to try my to☐ee,' said Ji☐.
The railway builders leve☐ed the land, then shove☐ed the earth out of the tu☐el.
Ro☐ert had a☐most a☐ his sums right, but number e☐even was rea☐y di☐icult.
The ma☐iage of the prince☐ ut the pa☐ace was a bri☐iant o☐a☐ion. She a☐eared on the te☐ace to wave.
The doctor re☐re☐ed he had forgo☐en the a☐ointment.
'Have you lost your a☐etite? You've surely not had su☐icient to eat a☐ready?'
The a☐a☐ination of President Ke☐edy was one of the most wi☐fu☐ acts of a☐re☐ion ever co☐i☐ed.

11 Sounds like 1

Twins

Find a pair of words that sound nearly the same as each other, to answer the clues given below. Both answers begin with the same letter.

Clue 1	Clue 2	Answer 1	Answer 2
A kind of tree	A sandy place	b *eech*	b *each*
A pointed stick	A juicy bit of meat	s............	s............
A fruit	Two things the same	p............	p............
Teacher .... a story	The bell was	t............	t............
Taller	To rent (e.g. a car)	h............	h............
Eye...........	Building	s............	s............
Trees have them	Actors make them	b............	b............
Short word for 'certain'	It's by the sea	s............	s............
Lots of cows	A noise was	h............	h............
Your middle	To squander	w............	w............

Rhymers

Pretend you are writing a poem. Find a word that rhymes with the word on the left, which also answers the clue on the right.

Sounds like	Clue	Answer
pour	Noise of a lion	*roar*
thick	Fast	....
roll	You put fruit in it	....
heard	Next after the second	....
Mary	Where milk is bottled	....
talk	Long-legged bird	....
drum	Tiny bit of bread	....
twist	Part of your arm	....
grain	Flies in the sky	....

12 Endings

Make changes to the ends of the words on the left, to follow the pattern of the example.

jump	jumps	jumping	jumped
hop	....	....	....
try	....	....	....
fill	....	....	....
file	....	....	....
pedal	....	....	....
lie	....	....	....
prance	....	....	....
cool	....	....	....
dial	....	....	....

Find words ending in either **ant** or **ent** that fit these clues: a 'key word' is given each time to help.

Key word	Clue	Answer
assist	Someone who works in a shop	....
differ	Not the same	....
study	Someone who studies	....
ignore	Someone who knows very little is	....
oppose	Someone against you, say in football	....
excel	Outstanding	....

Now find words ending in either **ance** or **ence** to fit these clues:

Key word	Clue	Answer
correspond	The clerk sorted the	....
enter	The way in	....
attend	Teacher checks this each day	....
offend	An action against the law	....
obey	Doing as you are told is	....
neglect	Being thoughtless and careless is	....

13 Changems

You may not find these quite as easy as you expect. You start with a word, then change one letter to make a word that fits the next clue. **(You might have to do some rearranging of the letters.)** Look at **all** the clues to help you throughout. The first one is started for you.

Starter: clip
You *clap* your hands
What a flag does in wind ...... *flap* ...
A small map ...... *plan* ...
Very faint in colour ...... *pale* ...
On an orange ....
Kind of jump ....
On a plant ....

Starter: rash
Hurry: run ....
To shove ....
You buy things there ....
A pork- ....
Fried potato ....
Not poor ....
Rainbow makes one ....

Starter: beech
By the sea: sandy ....
To get to, or arrive ....
Someone who doesn't play fair ....
Not dear ....
End of war brings it ....
Small part of something ....
The cost of something ....

Starter: pail
Dogs wag it ....
What trains run on ....
Falls from the sky: wet ....
Proud ....
Carries blood round you ....
Brides wear one ....
Opposite of death ....

Starter: fare
Has roundabouts and stalls ....
Two the same ....
Sort of fruit ....
It comes when you cry ....
Sort of big rabbit ....
On your head ....
Charles is Elizabeth's ....

Starter: eight
Opposite of black ....
Two times, not once ....
To put on paper ....
Tall building ....
The way to somewhere ....
What a volcano does ....
A short peace ....

14 ti, ci or si?

These clues are for words which have **ti**, **ci** or **si** in them, standing for a **sh** sort of sound – as in **action**.

Measles is this   in _ _ _ _ _ _ _
Lovely to eat   de _ _ _ _ _ _ _
Very, very old   a _ _ _ _ _ _
Very valuable   pr _ _ _ _ _ _
Cruel   vi _ _ _ _ _
Very careful   ca _ _ _ _ _ _
A close look   in _ _ _ _ _ _ _ _

He does tricks   ma _ _ _ _ _ _
A new product   in _ _ _ _ _ _ _
A loud bang   ex _ _ _ _ _ _ _
A country   na _ _ _ _
A real muddle   con _ _ _ _ _ _
A revolt   re _ _ _ _ _ _ _ _
Lots of space   s _ _ _ _ _ _ _

Silent letters

In the words that answer the clues below, there is at least one letter that is not sounded when the word is read.
These are all to do with your body:

Half way down your leg   _ _ _ _
On your hand   th _ _ _
Legs and arms are   l _ _ _ _

Between hand and arm   _ _ _ _ _
3 on each finger   _ _ _ _ _ _ _ _
'It's so cold I'm   n _ _ _.'

Now two animals with silent letters:

A young sheep   _ _ _ _

Tiny British bird   _ _ _ _

And a mixture:

Sung in church   _ _ _ _
A kind of elf   _ _ _ _ _

Used on hair   _ _ _ _
Make things with needles   _ _ _ _

Fill in the staircase with words containing silent letters.

Sounds like the opposite of **old**
It's the opposite of **right**
A war plane — B
Mends burst pipes
The angry giant was .... his teeth
Rhymes with **giggling**: to squirm about

15 Useful groups

Animals

Easy ones to start with! They all appear in cartoons.

Tom is one   c.............................   Jerry is one   m.............................

Daffy is one   d.............................   Bugs is one   r.............................

Now try these:

A small hen   c.............................   Fierce with stripes   t.............................

Has long trunk   e.............................   Has long neck   g.............................

Very fast   c.............................   Very slow   t.............................

Numbers

If you spell the answers to the clues properly, a number will appear in the crossword. reading downwards.

$54 \div 9$

$12 + 5 - 14$

$144 \div 12$

$5 \times 5 - 15$

$100 - 99$

$14 \times 2 - 20$

$132 \div 12$

$(16 + 5) \div 3$

$200 - 191$

Family words

The Goodall family consists of Mum, Dad, Diana and Robert. Dad has a brother called William; Mum has a sister called Penny. Penny has a child called Sarah. Now try these:

Mum and Dad are Diana's p.............   Dad is Robert's f.............................

Diana is her Mum's d.............   Robert is his Dad's s.............................

Penny is Robert's ....   William is Diana's ....

Robert is Penny's ....   Diana is Penny's ....

Sarah is Robert's ....   Penny's dad is Sarah's ....

16 Fillemups 2

Peg had a d _ _. His n _ _ _ was S _ _ t. Spot li _ _ _ to s _ _ by the o _ _ n d _ _ r at the b _ _ k of the ho _ _ _, to see if Peg would t _ _ _ him for a w _ _ k. In Sp _ _ _ _, they liked to go to the w _ _ ds. There was a p _ _ d in the woods. Du _ _ s s _ _ m on it, and Peg too _ s _ _ _ br _ _ d for them. She s _ _ d to Spot that he m _ _ t not b _ _ k at them, or they would fl _ a _ _ _.

When the holi _ _ _ _ came, Spot c _ _ _ d not go with the fam _ _ _, bec _ _ _ _ they went abr _ _ d. Inst _ _ _ he st _ _ _ d at some ke _ _ _ _ s near his home. At first, he gr _ _ _ _ d at being left al _ _ _, but after a short wh _ _ _, he settled, and qu _ _ _ enjo _ _ d being with the other an _ _ _ _ s. When Peg ret _ _ _ _ d to f _ _ _ h him, he became very n _ _ _ y, yapping and bo _ _ _ _ _ g about because he was so pl _ _ _ _ d to see her. 'You see, he didn't f _ _ _ _ t me,' she said. 'He k _ _ _ s who loves him.'

One e _ _ _ _ _ g, everyone had gone up _ _ _ _ _ s to bed. The night was si _ _ _ _, and the sky was da _ _ _ _ t black. Spot began wh _ _ _ _ g, then barked very l _ _ _ ly. Peg hu _ _ _ ed down. 'Stop fus _ _ _ g,' she cried. But Spot ca _ _ _ ed on. Peg ga _ _ d towards the n _ _ t house. Some _ _ _ _ g was badly w _ _ _ g. 'They are all away, vi _ _ _ ing fr _ _ _ ds. I'm going to p _ _ _ _ the po _ _ _ _ _.' She di _ _ _ ed 999 wh _ _ _ t Spot sat qu _ _ _ ly by. When the policemen came, they very se _ _ _ bly st _ _ _ _ d their car some dis _ _ _ _ e from the house.

Four police o _ _ _ _ _ rs cl _ _ _ ed out of the car. They ap _ _ _ _ _ _ ed cau _ _ _ usly. Two covered the front ent _ _ _ _ e, two the back. The intr _ _ _ _ s had no other pos _ _ _ _ e e _ _ t. Presently, the sliding p _ _ _ _ doors were opened. It was the bur _ _ _ _ _ s! The officers stepped up to them, and ar _ _ _ _ _ d them. Spot barked fur _ _ _ _ ly. He was proud because he had al _ _ _ _ d Peg, and she had man _ _ _ d very well in a dif _ _ _ _ lt situation.

17 Proof reading

When a book is published, it is first 'proof read' to check for any mistakes in the printing. This page needs another check. See how many mistakes you can find and put them right. The proper word always begins with the same letter as the wrong word.

On day, on the ~~whey~~ *way* to scool, I saw sum littel pufs of smoak comming form the widow of a howse acorss the rode. Their was no-one els arownd juts then. I crossd quikly, and ratled the door nob reely hard, and shoutted lowdly. There was on replie. I through smorl pebles from the graden at the window. Agen, no reply. I new it wood be foollish to trie enything moor by myself, so I hurryed to the neckst horse, and explaned how wurried I was. The oner braught a spear key, and we entred the propurty. He tolled me a daef gentelman lived there. I clozed the door to pervent a draft from makeing the fire wurse, and remaned at the foot of the stiars wilst my freind inspekted the badrooms. He shoutted that papper was smoldiering in a bakset, but it wasn't seriuos. There was no raisin to tellyfone the fire birgade. We could manedge things safly ourselfs. I slimed the stars, with a damp hankercheif round my face, becuase the smoke was quiet sevear, and together we raysed the old man, and carryed him onto the lending.

I was, of corse, late for school, but when my teatcher herd the reason, she ecsuses me. Latter in the day, the old man same to school, and was aloud into my class. In frunt of everboddy he torked about my bravry, and at the end of the weak their was a short peace in the newspapper about my aksion.

18 Useful groups

Days of the week

What a strange week! Put the spellings right.

Chewsday .... Mumday ....

Whensday .... Fursday ....

Fryday .... Sonsday ....

Satterday ....

Months of the year

Three months ending in **-ember**   ....

Two months ending in **-uary**   ....

Two *other* months beginning with **J**   ....

Two months beginning with **M**   ....

Two months beginning with **A**   ....

The other one!   ....

Still about months: you have to change one letter, and then rearrange the letters to make a month.

chasm .... paler ....

The seasons

The hottest .... The coldest ....

Things dying .... Things growing ....

Time

As you go round the clock, the length of time gets longer.

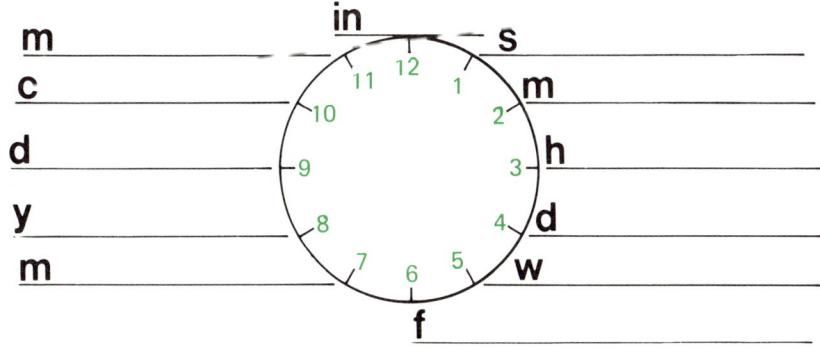

19 The wheel of fortune 2

This works like the first wheel: you **must** use the letters inside, and combine them with as many letters from the outside as you like. These are a little harder, so there are some clues to get you started.

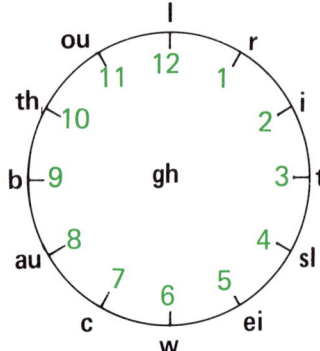

Opposite of 'wrong' ....

A number   e ....

Comes with a cold   c ....

The policeman .... the burglar red-handed.

Not smooth ....

Now make up your own.

A sudden wind ....

Inside your mouth ....

On a train: waves a flag ....

A villain ....

The Black death was one ....

Now add some of your own.

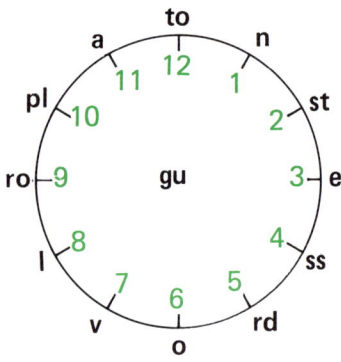

As some of these are quite hard, the first letter and the number of letters are given.

Small, but can cause malaria (m,8)

....

3 × 2 and 5 + 1 are (e,5) ....

A knight's companion (s,6) ....

Very old (a,7) ....

To overcome a country (c,7) ....

....

What's the longest word you can make?

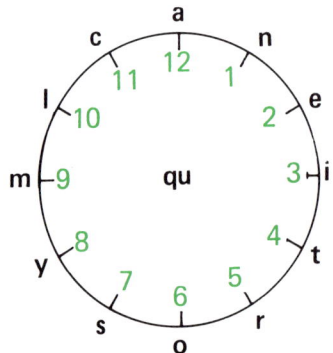

20 Sounds like 2

Twins

Fill the gaps in these sentences. The missing words both begin with the same letter, and they sound very similar.

It's cold: you must w.................. your coat. W.................. have you put it?

The teacher told the children to be qu.................. qu..................

Give me a p.................. of chocolate, and I will give you some p..................

Did you hear on the news w.................. the w.................. will be warm today?

The bank had to c.................. if the £1,000 c.................. was genuine or not.

'Do you do much football p..................?' 'Yes, I p.................. every day.'

The angry lad th.................. a stone th.................. the window.

A c.................. is a dried grape. A river may have a dangerous c..................

In each line below, the two words sound very like each other.

Word one		Word two	
An army officer	c..........................	Inside a nut	k..........................
A fight between two	d..................	A precious stone	j..........................
Comes from volcanoes	l................	A caterpillar is one	l......................
Elijah was one	p..........................	Money from selling	p....................

Rhymers

Rhymes with	Clue	Answer
motion	A large sea	o..........................
dutiful	Very lovely	b..........................
fried	Kind of dog blind people have	g..........................
thrilled	To construct something	b..........................
off	Animals eat from it	t..........................
kind	He .... the letter	s..........................
shoes	A mark on you from a blow	b..........................
smile	In church, the bride walks up it	a..........................

21 Beginnings

Many words begin with the same group of letters. Here are some fairly hard ones for you.

para- Useful if you fall from a plane (9) ....
  ═══ These 2 lines are (8) ....
  ⃞ This shape is a (13) ....
  Some unfortunate people are (9) ....

cata- A list of books, or things for sale (9) ....
  A terrible event (11) ....
  A kind of boat with two hulls (9) ....

pro- Not an amateur (12) ....
  To take someone to court (9) ....

con- To give great attention to something (11) ....
  To take away property (teacher might) (10) ....
  To give (to an appeal) (10) ....

contra- To say the opposite to someone (10) ....
  Smuggled goods (10) ....

inter- To meddle in something (9) ....
  'Please don't .... when I speak.' (9) ....

ad- Put in a newspaper to sell something (13) ....
  'The price of .... to the show is £5,' (9) ....

sym- A long piece of music (8) ....
  Helpful and kind (11) ....
  You describe these to your doctor (8) ....

We can often put a few letters at the beginning of a word to make an **opposite**: '**un**certain' means the opposite of 'certain'.
Here are some of these prefixes: **un, in, im, ir, dis**
Choose the right one each time to turn each word below into its **opposite**. Write the whole new word in the space.

sure .... appear .... patient ....
comfort .... comfortable ....
regular .... infect ....

22 Some harder groups

At the zoo

A tiger with spots? (7) l...................... Black and white stripes (5) z..............
Like a crocodile (9) a........................ Fierce: one horn (10) r......................
Long word for 'chimp' (10) ....
Enormous: loves mud (12) h..

At the hospital

Jack had an a.................. on his bicycle, so he went to the ca..................
department of the hospital. The su.................. examined him, and said he would need a small op.................., but it could be done without an ana..................

    Jack had been to hospital twice before – once to have a vac.................. and once with pn...................... Then he had had a very high t...................... but some excellent med.................. had brought it down.

    Even when i...................... was put on his wound as an ant......................, Jack kept quiet, and the nurse said he was a splendid pa..................

About eating

Peas and beans are (10) v .... Put on breakfast toast (9) m ....
Hot water and oats make it (8) p .... Used in salads (7) l..............................
Sounds rather like 'salary' (6) c .... Italian food (9) s ....
Wheat and barley are (7) ce.............. A salad dressing (10) m ....

About music

These are anagrams of words to do with music:

EXPOHONLY .... CLEARTIN ....
BENTROOM .... HENSOAPOX ....
PERTMUT .... MYSLABC ....

23 Fill it up – and put it right

This should make you think. Not only do you have to fill in the gaps, but you also have to keep an eye open for the spelling mistakes, and correct them.

Holidays

In sumer, we sumtimes take tr _ _ s to the see, to pl _ _ on the sa _ _ , s _ _ m in the watter, and ly in the son on our towles. Ne _ _ yaer, our hollyday will be aboard. We shall be traveling for sevral days th _ _ _ _ h the continant, stoping at n _ _ _ t in hotals along the root. We thaught about toeing the car _ _ _ n, but de _ _ _ _ d that the journey ac _ _ _ s the mountains might be rather dangerus with such a lode.

The most intersting and ex _ _ _ _ ng howiday in my experiance was a climing one. I did not ac _ _ _ _ any my family. Insted, I sh _ _ _ d acomadation in a large dormitry with other childern.

Our instructors were briliant climbers, and giuded us safly through the perliminery stages untill we were prep _ _ _ d to tackel the more dif _ _ _ _ _ t asents.

Because we had been taut so th _ _ _ _ _ _ ly we were only slihtly ap _ _ _ h _ _ _ _ ve as we gazed into the termendous drops between the cliffs.

One of my favorite hobbies is ph _ _ _ _ _ _ _ hy, and I was pursuaded to excibit ecxamples of my handiwork in a colection of holiday pictures aranged by our local lib _ _ _ _ an. I was extreemley delited when I le _ _ _ _ d that I had been awarded a speshul commandation by the Presi _ _ _ t of our local photographic socity.

24 So you want some harder ones?

These have ex in them:

Absolutely tired out (9) .... The way out (4) ....

An important test (11) .... A display (10) ....

Scientists do these (11) .... It breaks the rule (9) ....

These have sc in them:

Used for cutting (8) .... Islands near England (6) ....

To go down (d,7) .... The Queen has one (7) ....

Knocked out (u,11) ....

Makes you feel guilty (c,10) ....

These have ph in them:

Has no parents (o,6) .... A very big success (t,7) ....

Ruled Egypt, long ago (P,7) .... Had a wonderful coat (J,6) ....

A,B,C are part of it (a,8) .... Large animal (e,8) ....

These are unusual: they start with hy:

A springtime flower (8) .... An animal (5) ....

You sing it (4) .... An explosive gas (8) ....

These are a mixture. To help you, ex, sc, ph, or hy are put in the proper place in the word.

Please will you sign my _ _ _ _ _ _ _ ph book.

Toad thought out a wonderful sc _ _ _ _ to escape from prison.

John's contains a punctuation mark called an _ _ _ _ _ _ ph _ .

A dash between two parts of a word is a hy _ _ _ _ .

My back feels awful. Do you think I have sc _ _ _ _ _ _ ?

Don't ex _ _ _ _ _ _ _ _ : you only scored *one* goal.

If we have a mixture of things, we might call it _ _ sc _ _ _ _ _ _ _ _ _ .

Spelling banks

Because these spelling lists are of roughly equal difficulty, they can be used to make an endless series of tests by taking one word from each line. So you could have **in**, **kit**, **van**, **bar**, **sack**, **spit** and so on. They should **not** be used as lists to be learned by heart, but rather as checks made from time to time to see what progress is being made. Say the word, then put it into a sentence, then say it again on its own. Scores can be recorded on the progress chart on page 32.

at	in	on	up	and
pig	jet	kit	cot	fun
yet	bed	cub	van	fox
her	fur	for	sir	bar
pick	sack	rock	deck	quick
spit	drum	brim	black	slip
swim	skin	pram	brook	shook
all	well	ill	full	roll
bold	fold	look	spoon	sheets
spray	streak	sweep	teach	cloak
loaf	chest	stage	rage	aged
splash	shine	string	blinded	foolish
spokes	bread	breath	outlaw	hours
traffic	apple	butter	shopping	ladder
whistle	whole	window	owner	hoping
stalking	broken	fetched	weighing	themselves
brightly	appeared	priest	headache	fierce
cruising	presently	whiskers	armies	applies
plumber	scratches	accident	surprising	crumbling
armour	interval	appearance	shield	wrestle
knives	potatoes	volcanoes	calves	fairies
toughened	favourite	ghosts	negligence	thoughtfully
receipt	cinema	expression	examination	exclamation
exceptional	gnome	emphasize	thoroughly	impatiently

Scoring for spelling banks

Age	Average score out of 24
7	7–10
8	11–14
9	15–18
10	19–21

Short test of individual words

Working across the lines, say the word, then put it in a sentence, then say it again on its own.

is	was	has	one	here
what	your	why	could	said
many	young	woman	world	because
done	honey	fault	picnic	island
acid	engine	people	whose	poetry
beauty	future	height	neighbour	straight
machine	area	tongue	hymn	seize
route	social	daughter	occasion	souvenir

Dictation sentences

Read each sentence straight through to the child, then present groups of two or three words at a time, finally reading the sentence through once more. If he or she has made errors in three consecutive sentences, there is little point in continuing at that time.

1. We will go to the town this week.
2. When we are there, we will look in the shops.
3. I shall ask my dad to make a pond for some goldfish in our garden.
4. My aunt has a house with a window which looks out over a river.
5. The lucky children were the first people to see the Queen.
6. The teacher could not understand what had happened to her classroom.
7. The hospital nurse had a gentle touch.
8. I did not expect my friend to forget his promise.
9. After the circus, I won a toy elephant on the coconut stall.
10. The judge said he was puzzled as to how exactly to settle the question before him.
11. The bungalow was pleasantly decorated, without being beautiful.
12. Submarines which surface too soon may face a dangerous situation.

Scoring for individual word test

Age	Average number correct
7	15–18
8	19–22
9	23–26
10	27–30
11	31–34

Scoring for dictation sentences

Count the number of sentences in which the child has made no error, and then refer to the table below:

Age	Average sentences without error
7	3
8	5
9	7
10	9

Notes for parents and teachers

This book can be used to check on the 'symptoms' of spelling shown by your child – to give a diagnosis of his or her spelling strengths and weaknesses.

Although spaces are provided for answers in most of the exercises, you might prefer to have a separate book in which initial work is done. This will allow further attempts to be made on material that at first proves difficult. There is no reason why, on these first attempts, a dictionary should not be used. Several of the exercises give initial letters, and practice in finding words can only help general English skills. Later work on the same pages can be done in this book without the dictionary. Your child should be allowed to sample the pages, without feeling that he or she must finish one before the next. By seeing what level can be reached, you will be able to assess how far the 'spelling situations' outlined overleaf have been mastered.

In looking at your child's work, the following general points may be helpful:

Watch for an awareness that the same sound can be conveyed by different groups of letters (as in **hail** and **whale**) and that the same group of letters may represent different sounds (as in **friend** and **fiend**).

Look for indications of understanding not only of rules for letter combinations (such as the hoary '**i** before **e** except after **c**') but also of the fact that there are often exceptions (as in **seize** and **rein**). Look also for knowledge of rules for grammatical changes, into plurals, different tenses, and for the use of endings such as **-ing, -ly** and **ful**.

More specifically, you may like to check progress against the spelling situations outlined on the next page, which summarise many of the letter combinations and 'rules' to be mastered. The Spelling banks on pages 29–30 will be helpful here, as they contain the majority of simple combinations needed. The short test on page 30 can be used to check on knowledge of less regular combinations.

Progress chart

The grid below outlines the main areas in spelling practice covered by this book, and their relevant page numbers. Areas completed and learnt can be ticked off to show progress.

1 Different letter groups which can be used for similar sounds						
	-tch,-ch	-dge,-ge	-le,-el,-al	-ant,-ent	-er,-or,-ar	-si,-ti,-ci
page no.	4	4	10	15	11	17

2 The same letter groups which can be used for different sounds				
	ei	ie	ch	au
page no.	11	7,11	7	5

3 The use of double letters		
	ll,bb,ff,mm,rr,tt	pp,cc,dd
page no.	13	13

4 The use of silent letters	
	wr,kn,gn,mb etc.
page no.	17

5 Beginnings		
	in,im,un,ir,dis	para etc.
page no.	24	24

6 Change of endings		
		-y	-e
page no.	15	15

7 Special letter groups				
	qu	gh	ph	ex
page no.	22	22	27	27

8 Plurals	
	adding -s, adding -es,-f,-y
page no.	12

The various games (Wheel of Fortune, Changems and Fillemups) and the Spelling banks can also be used to check on knowledge of the above areas.

Record of Spelling bank work (colour in your scores)

Date	Age	0–5	6–10	11–15	16–20	21–24
....	....					
....	....					
....	....					
....	....					
....	....					